AMERICAN BAR ASSOCIATION
Commission on
Disability Rights

AMY ALLBRIGHT

THE ADA AMENDMENTS ACT AND THE EEOC'S IMPLEMENTING REGULATIONS

QUESTIONS AND ANSWERS

Cover by Kelly Book/ABA Publishing.

Printed in the United States of America

17 16 15 14 13   5 4 3 2 1

Library of Congress Cataloging-in-Publication Data

Allbright, Amy.

The ADA Amendments Act and the EEOC's implementing regulations : questions and answers / by Amy Allbright, Commission on Disability Rights, American Bar Association.

pages cm

ISBN 978-1-62722-145-0

1. United States. ADA Amendments Act of 2008--Miscellanea. 2. People with disabilities--Legal status, laws, etc.--United States--Miscellanea. I. American Bar Association. Commission on Disability Rights. II. Title.

KF3469.A3282008A2 2013

346.7301'38--dc23

2013018489

The ADA Amendments Act . . . brings millions of our fellow citizens back where they belong: under the protection of the ADA. . . .

When Congress passed the original ADA . . . , we made a promise of equality to Americans living with disabilities. Today we uphold our commitment to that promise.

Statement by Congressman Steny H. Hoyer (D-MD) After President George W. Bush Signed ADA Amendments Act (Sept. 24, 2008)

Contents

Acknowledgments

I give special thanks to William D. Goren and Paula D. Pearlman for their substantive analysis and review of the booklet. William Goren, J.D., LL.M., is an attorney, consultant, and blogger whose practice focuses on the practical implementation of the Americans with Disabilities Act. He can be followed at www.williamgoren.com. Goren is the author of *Understanding the Americans with Disabilities Act* (3d ed. American Bar Association 2010), the fourth edition of which is due out in fall 2013. Paula Pearlman, Esq., is the Executive Director of the Disability Rights Legal Center in Los Angeles, as well as a Visiting Associate Professor at Loyola Law School. She currently sits on the American Bar Association's Commission on Disability Rights (CDR).

Special thanks also to Katherine H. O'Neil, CDR's Chair, and the Honorable Adrienne C. Nelson, CDR's Editorial Advisory Committee Chair, for their support of this project.

Preface

The American Bar Association's (ABA) longstanding commitment to fostering diversity and inclusion in the legal profession is embodied in its Goal III—the elimination of bias and the enhancement of diversity in the profession. As a Goal III entity, the Commission on Disability Rights (CDR) has a twofold mission: "To promote the ABA's commitment to justice and the rule of law for persons with mental, physical, and sensory disabilities and to promote their full and equal participation in the legal profession."

The CDR advocates for equal opportunities and equal rights for persons with disabilities to be educated; work; live independently; make their own decisions; access government services, private businesses, public accommodations, and telecommunications; and be free from exclusion, segregation, and discrimination. The CDR is also committed to eliminating bias, enhancing diversity, and advancing the full and equal participation of law students and lawyers with disabilities in the profession. We work tirelessly to eliminate bias, stigma, and prejudices often associated with disability and to support law firms, corporate counsel, state and local bars, and law schools in making disability a vital component of their diversity initiatives, activities, and awards.

It takes a broad coalition working consistently and effectively to implement and carry out the promise of the American with Disabilities Act Amendments Act (ADAAA). The act itself represents a collaborative effort. Individuals and groups representing the disability, civil rights, and business communities came together in order to restore broad coverage for persons with a wide range of physical and mental impairments that was intended by the ADA and to protect them from discrimination on the basis of their disabilities.

This booklet provides readers with a comprehensive analysis of the ADAAA and the Equal Employment Opportunity Commission's (EEOC) regulations implementing it. Key changes made to the ADA are discussed, with one of the most important being to the definition of "disability." Citations to statutes, regulations, and illustrative cases are included, as well as a table of cases. My hope is that the booklet will raise disability awareness and inspire readers to make disability a key component of their diversity efforts, as well as to work to eliminate the societal and attitudinal barriers that preclude persons with disabilities from fully and equally participating in society.

Introduction

This booklet provides a general overview of the ADA Amendments Act and the Equal Employment Opportunity Commission's final regulations implementing the ADAAA. The format is question and answer. Statutory and case citations are provided.

General Questions About the ADAAA

What is the ADA Amendments Act?

The ADAAA is a civil rights law that amends the Americans with Disabilities Act, which was signed into law by President George H.W. Bush on July 26, 1990.

When was the ADAAA enacted?

President George W. Bush signed the ADAAA into law on September 25, 2008.

When did the ADAAA take effect?

January 1, 2009.

Does the ADAAA apply retroactively to discriminatory acts that occurred before its effective date?

The law itself is silent as to retroactivity. However, every federal circuit court that has considered the issue—relying on two U.S. Supreme Court cases[1]—has held that the ADAAA does not have retroactive effect.[2] For instance, an Alabama federal court ruled that the ADA, rather than the ADAAA, applied where the plaintiff failed to create a factual issue as to whether he was actually terminated on September 1, 2008.[3] Note that where the alleged violations occurred before and continued after January 1, 2009, the ADAAA will apply to

1. *See* Landgraf v. USI Film Prods., 511 U.S. 244 (1994) (discussing when a statute would be deemed to be retroactive); Rivers v. Roadway Express, Inc., 511 U.S. 298 (1994) (discussing when statutory overruling of a U.S. Supreme Court decision would be deemed to be able to apply retroactively).

2. *See, e.g.*, Thornton v. United Parcel Serv., Inc., 587 F.3d 27, 35 n.3 (1st Cir. 2009); Weidow v. Scranton Sch. Dist., 460 F. App'x 181 (3d Cir. 2012); Cochran v. Holder, 436 F. App'x 227 (4th Cir. 2011); EEOC v. Agro Distrib., LLC, 555 F.3d 462, 469 n.8 (5th Cir. 2009); Milholland v. Sumner Cnty. Bd. of Educ., 569 F.3d 562, 565 (6th Cir. 2009); Fredricksen v. United Parcel Serv. Co., 581 F.3d 516, 521 n.1 (7th Cir. 2009); Nyrop v. Indep. Sch. Dist. No. 11, 616 F.3d 728, 734 n.4 (8th Cir. 2010); Becerril v. Pima Cnty. Assessor's Office, 587 F.3d 1162, 1164 (9th Cir. 2009); Hennagir v. Utah Dep't of Corrs., 587 F.3d 1255, 1261 n.2 (10th Cir. 2009); Lytes v. DC Water & Sewer Auth., 572 F.3d 936, 942 (D.C. Cir. 2009).

3. Morris v. Precoat Metals, 2012 WL 4727995 (N.D. Ala. Sept. 27, 2012).

those allegations dealing with conduct occurring after January 1, 2009.[4]

What entities does the ADAAA apply to?

The same entities that the ADA applied to: employers with fifteen or more full-time employees, state and local government services of any size with respect to nonemployment matters, and places of public accommodation.

Rules of Construction

Does the ADAAA invalidate or limit the remedies, rights, and procedures of federal or state/local laws that give persons with disabilities greater or equivalent protection to that provided by the ADAAA?

No.[5]

Does the ADAAA alter the standards for determining eligibility for benefits under state workers' compensation law or state and federal disability benefit programs?

No.[6]

---

4. *See* Smith v. Valley Radiologists Ltd., 2013 WL 132538 (D. Ariz. Jan. 10, 2013).

5. 42 U.S.C. § 12201(b) (2009).

6. *Id.* § 12201(e).

General Questions about the EEOC Regulations

When did the EEOC issue its final regulations implementing the ADAAA?

March 25, 2011.

When did these regulations take effect?

May 24, 2011.

What titles of the ADA and sections of the Rehabilitation Act do the regulations apply to?

Title I of the ADA and Section 501 of the Rehabilitation Act.[7]

What entities do the EEOC regulations cover?

Employers with fifteen or more employees, employment agencies, labor organizations (unions), and joint labor management committees.[8]

What is the purpose of the regulations?

The regulations clarify and provide guidance on the changes made in the ADAAA.

What goals do the regulations achieve?

The regulations establish standards for eliminating disability-based discrimination in the workplace, promote inclusion

---

7. 29 C.F.R. § 1630.1(2011).

8. *Id.* § 1630.2(b).

and fairness in the workplace, combat second-class citizenship of persons with disabilities, avoid humiliation and stigma, and promote human dignity by enabling qualified individuals with disabilities to participate in the workforce.[9]

Purpose of the ADAAA

Why did Congress amend the ADA?

Congress found that several of the U.S. Supreme Court's rulings narrowed the broad scope of protection for persons with disabilities in a way not intended by Congress when it passed the ADA. As a result, lower courts had found that many individuals with a variety of disabilities were excluded from coverage under the ADA.[10]

What is the purpose of the ADAAA?

The ADAAA's purpose is to "carry out the ADA's objectives of providing 'a clear and comprehensive national mandate for the elimination of discrimination' and 'clear, strong, consistent, enforceable standards addressing discrimination' by reinstating a broad scope of protection . . . under the ADA."[11]

---

9. Equal Employment Provisions of ADAAA, 76 Fed. Reg. 16,986 (Mar. 25, 2011).

10. Pub. L. No. 110-325, § 2(a)(4)-(7), 122 Stat. 3553 (2008).

11. *Id.* Section 2(b)(1).

How does the ADAAA accomplish this purpose?

The ADAAA does so primarily by redefining "disability" in a way that favors broad coverage. For instance, a South Dakota federal court, referring to this broad coverage, found that three employees, two with diabetes and one with coronary artery disease, were disabled under the ADAAA.[12]

Definition of "Disability"

Three-Prong Definition

How does the ADAAA change the definition of "disability"?

Although the ADAAA retains the ADA's three-prong definition, it redefines the statutory terms "substantially limits," "major life activities," and "regarded as" and adds a rule of construction that requires "disability" to be construed in favor of broad coverage, to the maximum extent permitted by the terms of the ADA.[13]

---

12. Nichols v. City of Mitchell, 2012 WL 5471159 (Bkrtcy. D.S.D. Nov. 9, 2012).

13. Pub. L. No. 110-325, § 4, 122 Stat. 3553 (2008).

What titles of the ADA do the changes to the disability definition apply to?

The changes apply to Title I (employment), Title II (public services), and Title III (public accommodations and services operated by private entities).

How do these changes affect how courts should evaluate these cases?

The courts' primary focus is no longer on whether the person's impairment is a covered disability. This issue should not demand extensive analysis as was required prior to the ADAAA. Rather, the focus is on whether the covered entity complied with its obligations and whether discrimination has occurred.[14]

What impact has the ADAAA had on cases?

In light of the ADAAA's mandate of broad coverage, courts have found impairments that previously might have been excluded to be covered disabilities. For example, in *Rico v. Xcel Energy, Inc.*,[15] a New Mexico federal court ruled that an employee's allegations—that his back condition rendered him unable to climb utility poles or lift more than sixty pounds, and that his employer recommended that he apply for long-term disability benefits—were sufficient to raise an inference that he was disabled at the time of his termination. Furthermore, many courts have declined to grant Rule 12(b)(6)[16]

---

14. 29 C.F.R. § 1630.1(c)(4).

15. 893 F. Supp. 2d 1165 (D.N.M. 2012).

16. Fed. R. Civ. P. 12(b)(6).

motions to dismiss for failure to allege facts that, if proven, would establish an impairment that "substantially limits" a major life activity.[17]

What is the ADA's three-prong definition of "disability"?

"Disability means . . .—

(A) a physical or mental impairment that substantially limits one or more major life activities of such individual;
(B) a record of such an impairment; or
(C) being regarded as having such an impairment. . . ."[18]

---

17. *See, e.g.*, Lapier v. Prince George's Cnty., Md., 2012 WL 1552780, at *7–8 (D. Md. Apr. 27, 2012) (holding that plaintiff's allegations that his blood disorder caused decreased oxygen in his blood were sufficient to state a claim that he had a covered disability); Johnson v. Farmers Ins. Exch., 2012 WL 95387, at *1 (W.D. Okla. Jan. 12, 2012) (holding that plaintiff's allegations that she suffered from sleep apnea were sufficient to state a claim that she had a covered disability); *see also* Farina v. Branford Bd. of Educ., 2010 WL 3829160, at *11 (D. Conn. Sept. 23, 2010) (stating that, under the ADAAA, "it is possible that even a relatively minor lifting restriction could qualify as a disability within the statute"), *aff'd*, 458 F. App'x 13 (2d Cir. 2011).

18. 42 U.S.C. § 12102(1)(A)–(C).

What U.S. Supreme Court cases interpreting the "disability" definition does the ADAAA reject?

Those cases that Congress rejects[19] are:

- *Sutton v. United Air Lines, Inc.*,[20] ruling that (1) "if a person is taking measures to correct for, or mitigate, a physical or mental impairment, the effects of those measures—both positive and negative—must be taken into account when judging whether that person is 'substantially limited' in a major life activity,"[21] and (2) a person seeking "regarded as" protection must show that the employer mistakenly believes that the person has a substantially limiting impairment that he or she does not have, or has "a substantially limiting impairment when, in fact, the impairment is not so limiting."[22]
- *Toyota Motor Manufacturing, Kentucky, Inc. v. Williams*,[23] holding that (1) the terms "substantially limits" and "major life activities" in the definition of "disability" "need to be "interpreted strictly to create a demanding standard for qualifying as disabled,"[24]

---

19. Pub. L. No. 110-325, § 2(b)(2)–(4), 122 Stat. 3553 (2008).
20. 527 U.S. 471 (1999).
21. *Id.* at 482.
22. *Id.* at 489.
23. 534 U.S. 184 (2002).
24. *Id.* at 197.

(2) "substantially limits" means "prevents or severely restricts" a person from performing a major life activity,[25] and (3) "major" means "activities that are of central importance to most people's daily lives."[26]

When does a person have a "record of" a disability?

A person can demonstrate a "record of" a disability by demonstrating that he or she has a history of, or has been misclassified as having, a mental or physical impairment that substantially limits one or more major life activities when compared to most people in the general population.[27]

Can individuals be covered under both the "record of" and "actual" prongs?

Yes. For instance, an Oklahoma federal court denied an employer's motion to dismiss under the ADAAA, finding that an employee sufficiently pled that her obstructive sleep apnea substantially limited her in the major life activity of sleeping, so as to support her claims that she had an actual and record of disability.[28] Coverage under both prongs will often occur with impairments that are episodic or in remission. For instance, a person whose cancer is in remission can

---

25. *Id.* at 198.

26. *Id.*

27. 29 C.F.R. § 1630.2(k)(1) & (2).

28. Johnson v. Farmers Ins. Exch., 2012 WL 95387 (W.D. Okla. Jan. 12, 2012).

show that he or she has a history of having an impairment that substantially limited normal cell growth, as well as that his or her impairment is substantially limiting when active.[29]

What impairments virtually always will be covered under the "actual" or "record of" prongs, making the required individualized assessment simple and straightforward?

These impairments, termed by the EEOC "predictable assessments," include deafness, blindness, intellectual disabilities, partially or complete missing limbs, mobility impairments requiring wheelchair use, autism, cancer,[30] cerebral palsy, diabetes, epilepsy, HIV, multiple sclerosis, muscular dystrophy, major depressive disorder, bipolar disorder, post-traumatic stress disorder, obsessive-compulsive disorder, and schizophrenia.[31] Many of the listed impairments substantially limit a major bodily function, which seems to be the simplest way to prove coverage.

---

29. 29 C.F.R. pt. 1630, App., Section 1630.2(k).

30. *But see* Fierro v. Knight Transp., 2012 WL 4321304 (W.D. Tex. Sept. 18, 2012) (ruling that an employee failed to plead facts giving rise to an inference that his adenoid cystic carcinoma substantially limits one or more of his major life activities).

31. 29 C.F.R. § 1630.2(j)(3)(iii).

Is a person with a "record of" disability eligible for reasonable accommodations?

Yes, absent undue hardship, if he or she can show that the accommodations are needed and related to the past disability.[32]

How does the ADAAA change the definition of "regarded as" disabled?

The ADAAA rejects court decisions that had required a person to show that he or she was regarded as being substantially limited in a major life activity, thereby eliminating a functional test and restoring Congress's original intent. Rather, the person must show that he or she "has been subjected to an action prohibited under this chapter because of an actual or perceived physical or mental impairment whether or not the impairment limits or is perceived to limit a major life activity."[33] Under the ADAAA, the employer has an affirmative defense: The physical or mental impairment is both transitory and minor.[34]

---

32. *Id.* § 1630.2(k)(3).

33. 42 U.S.C. § 12102(3)(A). *See, e.g.*, Jordan v. Forfeiture Support Assocs., 2013 WL 828496 (E.D.N.Y. Mar. 5, 2013) (ruling that a plaintiff with carpal tunnel syndrome alleged facts rendering plausible her claim that her employer regarded her as disabled). *But see* Baldwin v. Duke, 2012 WL 3564021, at *3 (W.D.N.C. July 13, 2012) (misinterpreting the new standard, stating: "It is enough that the perceived impairment is perceived to 'limit' (not 'substantially limit') a major life activity").

34. 42 U.S.C. § 12102(3)(B). *See, e.g.*, Valdez v. Minn. Quarries, Inc., 2012 WL 6112846 (D. Minn. Dec. 10, 2012).

For instance, a North Carolina federal court ruled that an employee sufficiently demonstrated that he was "regarded as" disabled. The employee offered evidence that his supervisor stated that the head of the nursing department believed that the employee had relapsed into drug addiction and should be terminated. This evidence also constituted direct evidence of discriminatory motive sufficient to overcome a motion for summary judgment.[35]

What are prohibited actions?

Such actions include the "refusal to hire, demotion, placement on involuntary leave, termination, exclusion for failure to meet a qualification standard, harassment, or denial of any other term, condition, or privilege of employment."[36]

---

35. Scott v. Presbyterian Hosp., 2012 WL 4846753 (W.D.N.C. Oct. 11, 2012).

36. 29 C.F.R. § 1630.2(l)(1).

Does a finding of "regarded as" coverage equate to a finding of liability?

No. An employer may have a defense, such as that the employee posed a direct threat to self or others.[37]

Is a person who only meets the "regarded as" disabled prong eligible for reasonable accommodations?

No.[38] For instance, in *Walker v. Venetian Casino Resort, LLC*,[39] although an employee presented sufficient evidence that she was "regarded as" disabled, her ADAAA claim failed because she could not demonstrate that she was

---

37. *Id.* § 1630.2(l)(2); 29 C.F.R. pt.1603, App, Section 1630.2(l). *See* Wells v. Cincinnati Children's Hosp. Med. Ctr., 860 F. Supp. 2d 469 (S.D. Ohio 2012) (finding that a genuine issue of material fact existed under the ADAAA regarding whether a hospital considered all available information in concluding that a nurse with gastrointestinal problems presented health and safety risk to others if she returned to work in critical airway unit); Wurzel v. Whirlpool Corp., 482 F. App'x 1, 9 (6th Cir. 2012) (finding an employer's determination that an employee suffering from Prinzmetal's angina posed a direct threat to his own safety and that of others in a plant was based on a reasonable medical judgment, defeating the employee's claim of an ADA violation in connection with work restrictions and an unpaid leave).

38. 42 U.S.C. § 12201(h).

39. 2012 WL 4794149 (D. Nev. Oct. 9, 2012). *But see* Wright v. Hyundai Motor Mfg., Ala., LLC, 2012 WL 2814153, at *8 (M.D. Ala. July 10, 2012) (finding that a plaintiff with shoulder, elbow, and knee injuries sufficiently showed that he was "regarded as" disabled, but then incorrectly evaluating his failure-to-accommodate claim).

qualified for her job absent accommodation. However, if a person is covered under the "regarded as" and/or "actual" and "record of" prongs, he or she is eligible for reasonable accommodations.[40]

What prong should be used where an individual does not require reasonable accommodations?

According to the EEOC, the "regarded as" prong should be used.[41] However, a plaintiff may want to plead an "actual" or "record of" disability to have a fallback position.

Impairment

What is a physical impairment?

"[A]ny physiological disorder or condition, cosmetic disfigurement, or anatomical loss affecting one or more body systems. . . ."[42]

---

40. Pub. L. No. 110-325, § 6(a)(1)(h), 122 Stat. 3553 (2008); 29 C.F.R. § 1630.2(o).

41. 29 C.F.R. § 1630.2(g)(3).

42. *Id.* § 1630.2(h)(1).

Is pregnancy an impairment under the ADAAA?

No, as pregnancy does not result from a physiological disorder. However, certain impairments resulting from pregnancy, such as gestational diabetes, may be a covered disability.[43]

What is a mental impairment?

"[A]ny mental or psychological disorder, such as an intellectual disability . . . , organic brain syndrome, emotional or mental illness, and specific learning disabilities."[44]

Substantial Limitation

Does the ADAAA define the term "substantial limitation"?

No. The ADAAA rejects *Toyota*'s interpretation of the term as requiring a greater degree of limitation than Congress intended, as well as the EEOC's definition of "significantly restricted."[45] However, the EEOC's final regulations list nine

---

43. 29 C.F.R. pt. 1630, App., Section 1630.2(h). *See, e.g.*, Nayak v. St. Vincent Hosp. & Health Care Ctr., Inc., 2013 WL 121838, at *2–3 (S.D. Ind. Jan. 9, 2013) (finding that plaintiff sufficiently alleged pregnancy and post-pregnancy complications that substantially limited the major life activity of working).

44. 29 C.F.R. § 1630.2(h)(2).

45. Pub. L. No. 110-325, § 2(a)(7) & (8), 122 Stat. 3553 (2008); Toyota Motor Mfg., Ky., Inc. v. Williams, 534 U.S. 184 (2002).

rules of construction for determining whether an impairment substantially limits a major life activity.[46]

What are these rules of construction?

In general, the term "substantially limits" must be broadly construed "in favor of expansive coverage" and "is not meant to be a demanding standard" for qualifying as being disabled.[47] The basis of comparison is "most people in the general population," instead of "similarly situated persons." In

46. 29 C.F.R. § 1630.2(j)(1)(i)–(ix). *See, e.g.*, Butler v. BTC Foods Inc., 2012 WL 5315034 (E.D. Pa. Oct. 19, 2012) (noting that under the ADAAA, "the term 'substantially limits' [is to be] interpreted and applied to require a degree of functional limitation that is lower than the standard for 'substantially limits' applied prior to the ADAAA"; the term "is not meant to be a demanding standard"; and an impairment does not have to prevent, or significantly or severely restrict, a person from performing a major life activity to be considered substantially limiting. Here, although depression may constitute a disability under the ADAAA, an employee merely alleged that he has been treated for depression for several years by seeing a psychologist and taking medication, but failed to allege any functional limitations caused by his depression).

47. 29 C.F.R. § 1630.2(j)(1)(i). *See, e.g.*, Gibbs v. ADS Alliance Data Sys., Inc., 2011 WL 3205779, at *3 (D. Kan. July 28, 2011) (finding some evidence that plaintiff's carpal tunnel syndrome affected her ability to perform manual tasks, and keeping in mind that this inquiry is not meant to be "extensive" or "demanding," the court concluded that genuine issues of material fact existed as to whether plaintiff was disabled under the ADAAA).

Johnson v. City of Murray,[48] for example, a Utah federal court ruled that an animal shelter employee was not disabled under the ADAAA, as she failed to show that she was substantially limited in the major life activity of sleeping as compared to the average person in the general population. Specifically, she failed to offer any evidence regarding the frequency or severity of her insomnia or nightmares that the court could use to make that comparison.

Additionally, an impairment does not have to prevent or significantly or severely restrict a person from performing a major life activity in order to be considered "substantially limiting." However, not every impairment will constitute a covered disability.[49]

The primary object of attention in ADA cases is whether the covered entity complied with its obligations, and whether discrimination occurred. The "substantially limits" determi-

---

48. 2012 WL 5473127 (D. Utah Nov. 9, 2012). *But see* Howard v. Pa. Dep't of Pub. Welfare, 2013 WL 102662, at *11 (E.D. Pa. Jan. 9, 2013) (finding that plaintiff produced evidence from which a reasonable jury could conclude that her fibromyalgia substantially limits her ability to walk, sleep, and perform manual tasks as compared to most people in the general population); Naber v. Dover Healthcare Assocs., Inc., 765 F. Supp. 2d 622, 646 (D. Del. 2011) (ruling that a question of fact existed as to whether plaintiff's previously diagnosed depression is the cause of her inability to sleep one or two nights a week, and whether that sleeplessness is substantially limiting as compared to the average person in the general population).

49. 29 C.F.R. § 1630.2(j)(1)(ii).

nation "should not demand extensive analysis."[50] It requires an individualized assessment.[51] Typically, scientific, medical, or statistical evidence is not required in comparing a person's performance of a major life activity to that of most people in the general population, although such evidence may be presented if appropriate.[52]

The "substantially limits" determination must be made without regard to the ameliorative (positive) effects of mitigating measures, except for ordinary eyeglasses or contact lenses[53] (i.e., "lenses that are intended to fully correct visual acuity or eliminate refractive error"[54]), or to whether measures exist but the individual chooses to forego their use.[55] However, ameliorative effects may be relevant in determining whether the individual is qualified, needs a reasonable accommodation, or poses a direct threat to safety.[56] By con-

---

50. *Id.* § 1630.2(j)(1)(iii). *See, e.g.,* Graham v. St. John's United Methodist Church, 2012 WL 5298156 (S.D. Ill. Oct. 25, 2012) (ruling that an employee with permanent brain damage that causes him difficulty articulating his thoughts, slowness to comprehend, and difficulty challenging anyone he views as a figure of authority had a covered disability under the ADAAA).

51. 29 C.F.R. § 1630.2(j)(1)(iv).

52. *Id.* § 1630.2(j)(1)(v).

53. *Id.* § 1630.2(j)(1)(vi).

54. 42 U.S.C. § 12102(4)(E)(iii)(I).

55. 29 C.F.R. pt. 1630, App., Section 1630.2(j)(1)(vi).

56. *Id.*

trast, nonameliorative (negative) effects of mitigating measures may be considered.[57]

Impairments that are episodic or in remission constitute a protected disability if, when active, they substantially limit a major life activity.[58] Examples include epilepsy, post-traumatic stress disorder, major depressive disorder, diabetes, and asthma.[59]

57. 29 C.F.R. § 1630.2(j)(4)(ii).

58. *Id.* § 1630.2(j)(vii); 42 U.S.C. § 12102(4)(D). *But see* Allen v. Southcrest Hosp., 455 F. App'x 827, 832 (10th Cir. 2011) (finding that plaintiff's migraines did not substantially limit the major life activity of caring for oneself when active "and treated with medication," despite ADAAA's repudiation of consideration of mitigating measures in determining coverage); Butler v. BTC Foods Inc., 2012 WL 5315034, at *3 (E.D. Pa. Oct. 19, 2012) (ruling that while "[a]n impairment that is episodic or in remission is a disability if it would substantially limit a major life activity when active," plaintiff failed to allege that his hernia was anything more than a one-time occurrence).

59. 29 C.F.R. pt. 1630, App., Section 1630.2(j)(1)(vii). *See, e.g.*, Feldman v. Law Enforcement Assoc. Corp., 779 F. Supp. 2d 472, 483 (E.D.N.C. 2011) (finding that multiple sclerosis, when active, constitutes a disability under the ADAAA); Medvic v. Compass Sign Co., LLC, 2011 WL 3513499, at *7 (E.D. Pa. Aug. 10, 2011) (finding that when plaintiff's stutter is active, it substantially limits his ability to communicate, sometimes rendering him totally incapable of communicating at all).

For instance, in *Angell v. Fairmount Fire Protection District*,[60] a Colorado federal court found that a fire chief's cancer, which was in remission, was a covered disability under the ADAAA, as cancer, when active, substantially limits the major life activity of a major bodily function, i.e., normal cell growth. Nonetheless, he failed to show that he was discriminated against based on his disability.

An impairment need only be "substantially limiting" with respect to one major life activity for an individual to have an actual or record of a disability.[61] Transitory *and* minor impairments are significant only as to the "regarded as" prong.[62]

What was the intent of these rules?

Through these rules, Congress reinforces that the term "disability" is to be construed broadly and rejects the U.S. Supreme Court's interpretation of the term "substantially limits." Note, however, that Congress does not define the term "substantially limits."

---

60. 2012 WL 5389777 (D. Colo. Nov. 5, 2012). *See also* Norton v. Assisted Living Concepts, Inc., 786 F. Supp. 2d 1173, 1185 (E.D. Tex. 2011) (finding remissive cancer is a disability under the ADAAA); Hoffman v. Carefirst of Fort Wayne, Inc., 737 F. Supp. 2d 976, 985–86 (N.D. Ind. 2010) (same); Chalfont v. U.S. Electrodes, 2010 WL 5341846, at *9 (E.D. Pa. Dec. 28, 2010) (unpublished) (same).

61. Pub. L. No. 110-325, § 3(4)(C), 122 Stat. 3553 (2008); *see also* 29 C.F.R. § 1630.2(j)(viii).

62. 29 C.F.R. § 1630.2(j)(ix).

What are mitigating measures?

Mitigating measures eliminate or reduce the symptoms or impact of an impairment. The ADAAA provides a *non-exhaustive* list of mitigating measures. These include medication; medical supplies, equipment, or appliances; low-vision devices (those that magnify, enhance, or otherwise augment a visual image); prosthetics; hearing aids, cochlear implants, or other implantable hearing devices; mobility devices; oxygen therapy equipment and supplies; use of assistive technology; reasonable accommodations or auxiliary aids or services; or learned behavioral or adaptive neurological modifications.[63] Auxiliary aids and services include "(A) qualified interpreters or other effective methods of making aurally delivered materials available to individuals with hearing impairments; (B) qualified readers, taped texts, or other effective methods of making visually delivered materials available to individuals with visual impairments; (C) acquisition or modification of equipment or devices; and (D) other similar services and actions."[64]

Is the "transitory and minor" determination subjective or objective?

The determination is objective.[65] Accordingly, the subjective beliefs of an employer are not relevant.

---

63. 42 U.S.C. § 12102(4)(E)(i)(I–IV).
64. *Id.* § 12102(1)(A–D).
65. 29 C.F.R. § 1630.15(f).

Can an impairment whose effects last (or are expected to last) fewer than six months be considered "substantially limiting"?

Yes, under the "actual" or "record of" disability prongs,[66] and under the "regarded as" prong if the condition is not such that it is both transitory (has an actual or expected duration of six months or less[67]) and minor.[68] Note that in the "substantial limitation" determination, an impairment's duration is a relevant factor to consider. "Impairments that last only for a short period of time are typically not covered, although they may be covered if sufficiently severe."[69]

---

66. *Id.* § 1630.2(j)(1)(ix).

67. 42 U.S.C. § 12102(3)(B).

68. 29 C.F.R. pt. 1630, App., Section 1630.2(j)(1)(ix). *See, e.g.*, Sam-Sekur v. Whitmore Grp., Ltd., 2012 WL 2244325 (E.D.N.Y. June 15, 2012) (ruling that plaintiff's breast cancer care, appendectomy, infection from an IUD, and infected oral implant were each "transitory and minor"); White v. Interstate Distrib. Co., 438 F. App'x 415, 420 (6th Cir. 2011) (plaintiff could not establish a "regarded as disabled" claim because he suffered a transitory impairment with a duration of one or two months); Dugay v. Complete Skycap Servs., Inc., 2011 WL 3159171 (D. Ariz. July 26, 2011) (three-month-long disability resulting from car accident was "transitory and minor"). *But see* Nayak v. St. Vincent Hosp. & Health Care Ctr., Inc., 2013 WL 121838, at *3 (S.D. Ind. Jan. 9, 2013) (finding that plaintiff's alleged pregnancy and post-pregnancy complications lasted more than six months and, thus, "transitory and minor" argument failed).

69. 29 C.F.R. pt. 1630, App., Section 1630.2(j)(1)(ix). *See, e.g.,* Wanamaker v. Westport Bd. of Educ., 2012 WL 4445314 (D. Conn. Sept. 25, 2012); Lewis v. Fla. Default Law Grp., 2011 WL 4527456 (M.D. Fla. Sept. 16, 2011).

Major Life Activities

What are major life activities?

The ADAAA provides an *illustrative, nonexhaustive* list of major life activities. These include: "caring for oneself, performing manual tasks, seeing, hearing, eating, sleeping, walking, standing, lifting, bending, speaking, breathing, learning, reading, concentrating, thinking, communicating, . . . working [and] the operation of a major bodily function"[70] (e.g., the immune system, normal cell growth, digestive, bowel, bladder, neurological, brain, respiratory, circulatory, endocrine, and reproductive functions). For instance, a Georgia federal court ruled that an employee's breast disease constituted a covered disability under the ADAAA, where it was the result of abnormal cell growth and abnormal endocrine and reproductive functioning.[71] Also, a Pennsylvania federal court found that, with regard to a plaintiff with chronic fatigue, it could not say "as a matter of law that 'waking up' is not a major life activity."[72] The court reasoned that "[i]f sleeping

70. 42 U.S.C. § 12102(2)(A) & (B). *See, e.g.*, Mercer v. Arbor E & T, LLC, 2013 WL 164107, at *13 (S.D. Tex. Jan. 15, 2013) (finding, in light of the "substantially limits" standard created by the ADAAA, that a factual issue existed whether a plaintiff's difficulty concentrating is unique, and unlike those experienced by the general population).

71. Coker v. Enhanced Senior Living, Inc., 2012 WL 4326429 (N.D. Ga. Sept. 18, 2012); *see, e.g.*, Meinelt v. P.F. Chang's China Bistro, Inc., 787 F. Supp. 2d 643, 651 (S.D. Tex. 2011) (denying employer summary judgment because plaintiff's brain tumor substantially limited brain functions).

72. Thomas v. Bala Nursing & Ret. Ctr., 2012 WL 2581057, at n.14 (E.D. Pa. July 3, 2012).

meets this standard, then it is hard to see how the opposite (waking up) would fail to."[73] The court pointed to the Third Circuit's characterization of a major life activity as one that is "inescapably central to anyone's life. *Taylor v. Phoenixville School Dist.,* 184 F.3d 296, 307 (3d Cir. 1999)."[74] With the addition of major bodily functions, many individuals will be covered, since impairments affect the functioning of body systems. For instance, cancer affects a person's normal cell growth; diabetes, the operation of pancreas and the function of endocrine system; and HIV, the immune system. The addition of major bodily functions was significant, as it better addresses chronic impairments and results in more expansive coverage.[75]

What activities did the EEOC regulations add to the ADAAA's list of major life activities?

The regulations added interacting with others, sitting, and reaching, as well as the major bodily functions of special-sense organs and skin, cardiovascular, hemic, lymphatic, and musculoskeletal.[76] These additions by the EEOC would need to be given deference by the court as the ADAAA specifi-

73. *Id.*

74. *Id.*

75. 29 C.F.R. pt. 1630, App., Section 1630.2(i). *See, e.g.,* Alexiadis v. N.Y. Coll. of Health Professions, 891 F. Supp. 2d 418 (E.D.N.Y. 2012)

76. 29 C.F.R. § 1630.2(i)(1)(i)–(ii).

cally gave the EEOC, as well as the department of justice, the authority to implement definitional terms.[77]

Does the operation of a major bodily function include the operation of an individual organ within a body system?

Yes; for instance, the operations of the kidney, liver, or pancreas.[78]

Can a person with a learning disability who has achieved a high level of success be substantially limited in the major life activity of learning?

Yes. The disability determination focuses on how a major life activity is limited, rather than on the outcomes a person can achieve. A person with a learning disability may, for instance, need to spend additional time or effort to read, write, or learn compared to most people in the general population.[79] For example, an Ohio federal court denied a medical school's motion for summary judgment, finding that a student sufficiently demonstrated that her attention deficit disorder (ADD) substantially limited her ability to learn.[80] Specifically, she presented evidence that her ADD affected

77. 42 U.S.C. § 12205a.

78. 29 C.F.R. § 1630.2(i)(1)(ii).

79. 29 C.F.R. pt. 1630, App., Section 1630.2(j)(1)(v).

80. Peters v. Univ. of Cincinnati Coll. of Med., 2012 WL 3878601 (S.D. Ohio Sept. 6, 2012).

her ability to learn and retain new information, and that she struggled with organizing her thoughts and registering information more than the average person. The court pointed out that the facts that she graduated from college with a dual degree and was able to succeed in part in medical school merely indicate that she was able to achieve some measure of success despite her disability. However, these facts "do not speak to her learning ability as compared with the average person. . . . Defendant's rationale—that anyone who has had some modicum of academic success cannot be found to have a disability that affects learning—flies in the face of Congress' directives and the relevant implementing regulations."[81]

What change did the regulations make regarding the major life activity of working?

The regulations moved the discussion of this major life activity from the main text to the interpretive appendix. The EEOC did so, pointing out that "no other major life activity was singled out in the regulations for elaboration,"[82] and that "this major life activity will be used in only very targeted situations" due to the expanded definition of "disability."[83] The EEOC explained that individuals with disabilities will in most instances be able to show a substantial limitation in a major activity other than work-

81. *Id.* at *6.

82. Equal Employment Provisions of ADAAA, 76 Fed. Reg. 16,984 (Mar. 25, 2011).

83. 29 C.F.R. pt. 1630, App., Section 1630.2(j).

ing, since impairments that substantially limit working usually substantially limit one or more other major life activities.[84]

Do the regulations make it easier to prove a substantial limitation in working?

Yes. Individuals must still prove a substantial limitation in the ability to perform a class or jobs or a range of jobs in various classes. However, the regulations emphasize that, in light of the ADAAA, the EEOC and the courts must apply a lower standard in determining a substantial limitation on a major life activity, including working. The regulations emphasize that "the terms 'class of jobs' and 'broad range of jobs in various classes' will be applied in a more straightforward and simple manner."[85] The regulations define the term "class of jobs" as the nature of the work that a person is limited to performing, such as clerical or law enforcement jobs, or the job-related requirements that a person is limited in meeting, such as repetitive lifting, bending, or reaching. For instance, an Illinois federal court ruled that an employee was substantially limited in a broad range of jobs, where he was unable to perform lifting tasks required for journeyman carpentry work.[86] By contrast, in *Johnson v. City of Murray*,[87] a Utah federal court ruled that an animal shelter employee

84. *Id.*

85. *Id.*

86. Chi. Reg'l Council of Carpenters v. Thorne Assocs., Inc., 893 F. Supp. 2d 952 (N.D. Ill. 2012).

87. 2012 WL 5473127 (D. Utah Nov. 9, 2012).

was not disabled under the ADAAA, as she failed to show that she was substantially limited in the major life activity of working. Although the court acknowledged the ADAAA's broader definition of "disability," it stated that the "broad class of jobs" restriction remains in place, yet failed to discuss the EEOC's interpretation of this term. The court went on to conclude that the employee's claims that she was unable to work with her supervisor and to perform her job while the office was understaffed is "only an argument that Plaintiff could not perform her specific job under specific circumstances."[88]

Generally, will individuals establish coverage by proving a substantial limitation in major life activities other than working?

Yes, because impairments that substantially limit working will invariably substantially limit one or more other major life activities.[89]

For the substantial limitation determination, may one consider the condition, manner, or

88. *Id.* at *21. *See also* Flynt v. Biogen Idec, Inc., 2012 WL4588570, at *5 (S.D. Miss. Sept. 30, 2012) (ruling that an employee with depression and anxiety was not substantially limited in working, where his sole contention was that he could not work with his supervisor—"certainly not a 'broad class of jobs' as he is required to show.").

89. 29 C.F.R. pt. 1630, App., Section 1630.2(j).

duration under which a major life activity can be performed?

Yes,[90] although this should be unnecessary in most cases. These concepts may mean the difficulty, effort, or time required to perform a major life activity; pain experienced when performing a major life activity; the length of time it takes to perform a major life activity; and/or the way an impairment affects the operation of a major bodily function.[91]

Can an individual without a disability file a claim that he or she was subject to discrimination because of lack of disability?

No, and this includes a claim that a person with a disability was granted an accommodation that was denied to a person without a disability. The regulations added this provision.[92]

Accommodations

What is a reasonable accommodation?

A reasonable accommodation can include "making existing facilities used by employees readily accessible to and usable by individuals with disabilities," as well as "job restructuring, part-time or modified work schedules, reassignment

---

90. 29 C.F.R. § 1630.2(j)(4).

91. *Id.* § 1630.2(j)(4)(ii).

92. Pub. L. No. 110-325, § 6(a)(1)(g), 122 Stat. 3553 (2008); 29 C.F.R § 1630.4(b).

to a vacant position, acquisition or modification of equipment or devices, appropriate adjustment or modifications of examinations, training materials or policies, the provision of qualified readers or interpreters, and other similar accommodations for individuals with disabilities."[93]

When is an accommodation not reasonable?

An accommodation is not reasonable if it imposes an "undue hardship," i.e., "an action requiring significant difficulty or expense."[94]

What factors should be considered in determining "undue burden"?

Factors include:

1. The nature and cost of the accommodation needed under this chapter;
2. The overall financial resources of the facility or facilities involved in the provision of the reasonable accommodation; the number of persons employed at such facility; the effect on expenses and resources, or the impact otherwise of such accommodation upon the operation of the facility;
3. The overall financial resources of the covered entity; the overall size of the business of a covered entity with

93. 42 U.S.C. § 12111(9)(A) & (B).

94. *Id.* § 12111(10)(A).

respect to the number of its employees; the number, type, and location of its facilities; and

4. The type of operation or operations of the covered entity, including the composition, structure, and functions of the workforce of such entity; the geographic separateness, administrative, or fiscal relationship of the facility or facilities in question to the covered entity.[95]

What are some benefits of accommodations attributable to the ADAAA and the EEOC regulations?

1. Increases employee retention
2. Increases employee productivity
3. Reduces absenteeism
4. Lowers turnover
5. Improves employee health
6. Eliminates costs associated with training new employees
7. Increases company diversity
8. Increases company morale
9. Increases profitability
10. Improves customer interactions
11. Increases workplace safety
12. Makes the accommodations process simpler for employers

---

95. *Id.* § 12111(10)(B)(i)–(iv).

13. Decreases the need for litigation of who is a "person with a disability"
14. Streamlines issues requiring judicial attention
15. Saves workers' compensation and other insurance costs
16. Stimulates the economy
17. Diminishes discrimination against qualified individuals, promoting human dignity and equity
18. Integrates and promotes contact with employees with disabilities, diminishing stereotypes and promoting design, availability, and awareness of accommodations
19. Enables persons with disabilities to reach their full potential[96]

96. Equal Employment Provisions of ADAAA, 76 Fed. Reg. 16,996–98 (Mar. 25, 2011).

Employer Qualification Criteria

What rule applies to employer's use of qualification standards, employment tests, or other selection criteria for persons with disabilities?

Employers are prohibited from using selection criteria that screens out (or tends to screen out) or otherwise deny a job or benefit to an individual with a disability, unless the criteria is job-related and consistent with business necessity, and if performance of the job cannot be accomplished by reasonable accommodation.[97]

What is the purpose of the rule?

The rule ensures that persons with disabilities are not excluded from job opportunities unless they cannot perform the job.[98] Accordingly, there must be a fit between the job criteria and the employee or applicant's ability to perform the job. For instance, an Illinois federal court ruled under the ADAAA that an applicant for a carpentry job and his union sufficiently pled that the employer's fitness for hire test administered by employer was neither job-related nor consistent with business necessity.[99] The test required appli-

97. 42 U.S.C. § 12113(a).

98. 29 C.F.R. pt. 1630, App., Section 1630.10(a).

99. Chi. Reg'l Council of Carpenters v. Thorne Assocs., Inc., 893 F. Supp. 2d 952 (N.D. Ill. 2012).

cants to lift and carry a fifty-pound box between sixteen and seventy-two inches vertically, as well as a one hundred-pound box to a height between six and fifty-six inches vertically. Plaintiffs alleged that the applicant was able to perform the same types of work he had performed for the employer in the past, and that the "test requirements were not realistic metric of tasks actually performed by carpenters in field."[100]

Does this rule apply if the criteria unintentionally screens out (or tends to screen out) persons with disabilities?

Yes.[101]

Are production standards subject to this rule?

Generally, no. The intent of the rule is not to second guess an employer's business judgment with regard to production standards.[102]

What is an example of criteria that is not consistent with business necessity?

Criteria that do not concern an "essential job function,"[103] defined as "the fundamental job duties of the employment position that the individual with a disability holds or

---

100. *Id.* at 960.

101. 29 C.F.R. pt. 1630, App., Section 1630.10(a).

102. *Id. See* 29 C.F.R. § 1630.2(n).

103. 29 C.F.R. pt. 1630, App., Section 1630.10(a).

desires."[104] For instance, the Ninth Circuit denied an employer summary judgment on the grounds that it failed to show that its breathilator test was job-related and a business necessity, and the test tended to screen out individuals with diabetes-related high blood pressure.[105] The employer failed to show that the test fairly and accurately measured the plaintiff's actual ability to perform the essential functions of his job as a metallurgy welding specialist. In particular, the employer did not show that the plaintiff carried a respirator, or that respirators were readily accessible in the areas where he was assigned to work. The plaintiff noted that in his twenty-three years he never used a respirator.[106]

Do "qualification standards" include a direct threat requirement?

Yes, an individual cannot pose a direct threat to the health or safety of others in the workplace.[107]

---

104. 29 C.F.R. § 1630.2(n)(1).

105. Rohr v. Salt River Project Agr. Improvement & Power Dist., 555 F.3d 850 (9th Cir. 2009).

106. *Id.* at 863.

107. 42 U.S.C. § 12113(b).

Can employers use uncorrected vision qualification standards, tests, or other selection criteria?

Yes, but only if the standards, tests, or criteria are job-related and consistent with business necessity.[108]

Can a person who has fully corrected vision with eyeglasses or contact lenses challenge such criteria?

Yes, as such a person still has an impairment.[109]

Can a person without a covered disability challenge such criteria?

Yes, if they are "adversely affected" by the application of the criteria to them.[110]

---

108. *Id.* § 12113(c).

109. 29 C.F.R. pt. 1630, App., Section 1630.10(b).

110. 29 C.F.R. § 1630.10(b).

Table of Cases

Alexiadis v. N.Y. Coll. of Health Professions, 891 F. Supp. 2d 418 (E.D.N.Y. 2012)

Allen v. Southcrest Hosp., 455 F. App'x 827 (10th Cir. 2011)

Angell v. Fairmount Fire Prot. Dist., 2012 WL 5389777 (D. Colo. Nov. 5, 2012)

Baldwin v. Duke, 2012 WL 3564021 (W.D.N.C. July 13, 2012)

Becerril v. Pima Cnty. Assessor's Office, 587 F.3d 1162 (9th Cir. 2009)

Butler v. BTC Foods Inc., 2012 WL 5315034 (E.D. Pa. Oct. 19, 2012)

Chalfont v. U.S. Electrodes, , 2010 WL 5341846 (E.D. Pa. Dec. 28, 2010) (unpublished)

Chi. Reg'l Council of Carpenters v. Thorne Assocs., Inc., 893 F. Supp. 2d 952 (N.D. Ill. 2012)

Cochran v. Holder, 436 F. App'x 227 (4th Cir. 2011)

Coker v. Enhanced Senior Living, Inc., 2012 WL 4326429 (N.D. Ga. Sept. 18, 2012)

Dugay v. Complete Skycap Servs., Inc., 2011 WL 3159171 (D. Ariz. July 26, 2011)

EEOC v. Agro Distrib., LLC, 555 F.3d 462 (5th Cir. 2009)

Farina v. Branford Bd. of Educ., 2010 WL 3829160 (D. Conn. Sept. 23, 2010)

Feldman v. Law Enforcement Assoc. Corp., 779 F. Supp. 2d 472 (E.D.N.C. 2011)

Fierro v. Knight Transp., 2012 WL 4321304 (W.D. Tex. Sept. 18, 2012)

Flynt v. Biogen Idec, Inc., 2012 WL 4588570 (S.D. Miss. Sept. 30, 2012)

Fredricksen v. United Parcel Serv. Co., 581 F.3d 516 (7th Cir. 2009)

Gibbs v. ADS Alliance Data Sys., Inc., 2011 WL 3205779 (D. Kan. July 28, 2011)

Graham v. St. John's United Methodist Church, 2012 WL 5298156 (S.D. Ill. Oct. 25, 2012)

Hennagir v. Utah Dep't of Corrs., 587 F.3d 1255 (10th Cir. 2009)

Hoffman v. Carefirst of Fort Wayne, Inc., 737 F. Supp. 2d 976 (N.D. Ind. 2010)

Howard v. Pa. Dep't of Pub. Welfare, 2013 WL 102662 (E.D. Pa. Jan. 9, 2013)

Johnson v. City of Murray, 2012 WL 5473127 (D. Utah Nov. 9, 2012)

Johnson v. Farmers Ins. Exch., 2012 WL 95387 (W.D. Okla. Jan. 12, 2012)

Jordan v. Forfeiture Support Assocs., 2013 WL 828496 (E.D.N.Y. Mar. 5, 2013)

Landgraf v. USI Film Prods., 511 U.S. 244 (1994)

Lapier v. Prince George's Cnty., Md., 2012 WL 1552780 (D. Md. Apr. 27, 2012)

Lewis v. Fla. Default Law Grp., 2011 WL 4527456 (M.D. Fla. Sept. 16, 2011)

Lytes v. DC Water & Sewer Auth., 572 F.3d 936 (D.C. Cir. 2009)

Medvic v. Compass Sign Co., LLC, 2011 WL 3513499 (E.D. Pa. Aug. 10, 2011)

Meinelt v. P.F. Chang's China Bistro, Inc., 787 F. Supp. 2d 643 (S.D. Tex. 2011)

Mercer v. Arbor E & T, LLC, 2013 WL 164107 (S.D. Tex. Jan. 15, 2013)

Milholland v. Sumner Cnty. Bd. of Educ., 569 F.3d 562 (6th Cir. 2009)

Morris v. Precoat Metals, 2012 WL 4727995 (N.D. Ala. Sept. 27, 2012)

Naber v. Dover Healthcare Assocs., Inc., 765 F. Supp. 2d 622 (D. Del. 2011)

Nayak v. St. Vincent Hosp. & Health Care Ctr., Inc., 2013 WL 121838 (S.D. Ind. Jan. 9, 2013)

Nichols v. City of Mitchell, 2012 WL 5471159 (Bkrtcy. D.S.D. Nov. 9, 2012)

Norton v. Assisted Living Concepts, Inc., 786 F. Supp. 2d 1173 (E.D. Tex. 2011)

Nyrop v. Indep. Sch. Dist. No. 11, 616 F.3d 728 (8th Cir. 2010)

Peters v. Univ. of Cincinnati Coll. of Med., 2012 WL 3878601 (S.D. Ohio Sept. 6, 2012)

Rico v. Xcel Energy, Inc., 893 F. Supp. 2d 1165 (D.N.M. 2012)

Rivers v. Roadway Express, Inc., 511 U.S. 298 (1994)

Rohr v. Salt River Project Agr. Improvement & Power Dist., 555 F.3d 850 (9th Cir. 2009)

Sam-Sekur v. Whitmore Grp., Ltd., 2012 WL 2244325 (E.D.N.Y. June 15, 2012)

Scott v. Presbyterian Hosp., 2012 WL 4846753 (W.D.N.C. Oct. 11, 2012)

Smith v. Valley Radiologists Ltd., 2013 WL 132538 (D. Ariz. Jan. 10, 2013)

Sutton v. United Air Lines, Inc., 527 U.S. 471 (1999)

Thomas v. Bala Nursing & Ret. Ctr., 2012 WL 2581057 (E.D. Pa. July 3, 2012)

Thornton v. United Parcel Serv., Inc., 587 F.3d 27 (1st Cir. 2009)

Toyota Motor Mfg., Ky., Inc. v. Williams, 534 U.S. 184 (2002)

Valdez v. Minn. Quarries, Inc., 2012 WL 6112846 (D. Minn. Dec. 10, 2012)

Wanamaker v. Westport Bd. of Educ., 2012 WL 4445314 (D. Conn. Sept. 25, 2012)

Weidow v. Scranton Sch. Dist., 460 F. App'x 181 (3d Cir. 2012)

Wells v. Cincinnati Children's Hosp. Med. Ctr., 860 F. Supp. 2d 469 (S.D. Ohio 2012)

White v. Interstate Distrib. Co., 438 F. App'x 415 (6th Cir. 2011)

Wright v. Hyundai Motor Mfg., Ala., LLC, 2012 WL 2814153 (M.D. Ala. July 10, 2012)

Wurzel v. Whirlpool Corp., 482 F. App'x 1 (6th Cir. 2012)